Did you know, more than three-quarters of Japan is rural – or countryside – but nine out of ten people live in the cities?
Yes! Over 37 million people live in Tokyo – more than in the whole of Australia and New Zealand combined!
まわりは関係ない。
納得するまで
やるかどうか。
作詞家 秋元康
しゃぶしゃぶバイキング
しゃぶ葉
コンタクト
Caféレストラン ガスト
109
SHIBUYA

# 2 KYUSHU

Our first stop is Kyushu Island in southern Japan. It has an active volcano, and many **hot springs**, called "onsen".

Some onsen in Beppu city are so hot, they're called "hells"! This one has red water! It's so hot you can cook food in the steam.

# 1 WELCOME TO JAPAN!

# Kiku and Kenji EXPLORE JAPAN

**CONTENTS**




Written by Mio Debnam

Illustrated by Nathalia Takeyama



**Collins**

Japan has 111 active volcanoes.

Volcanic steam smells eggy!

# 3 KYOTO

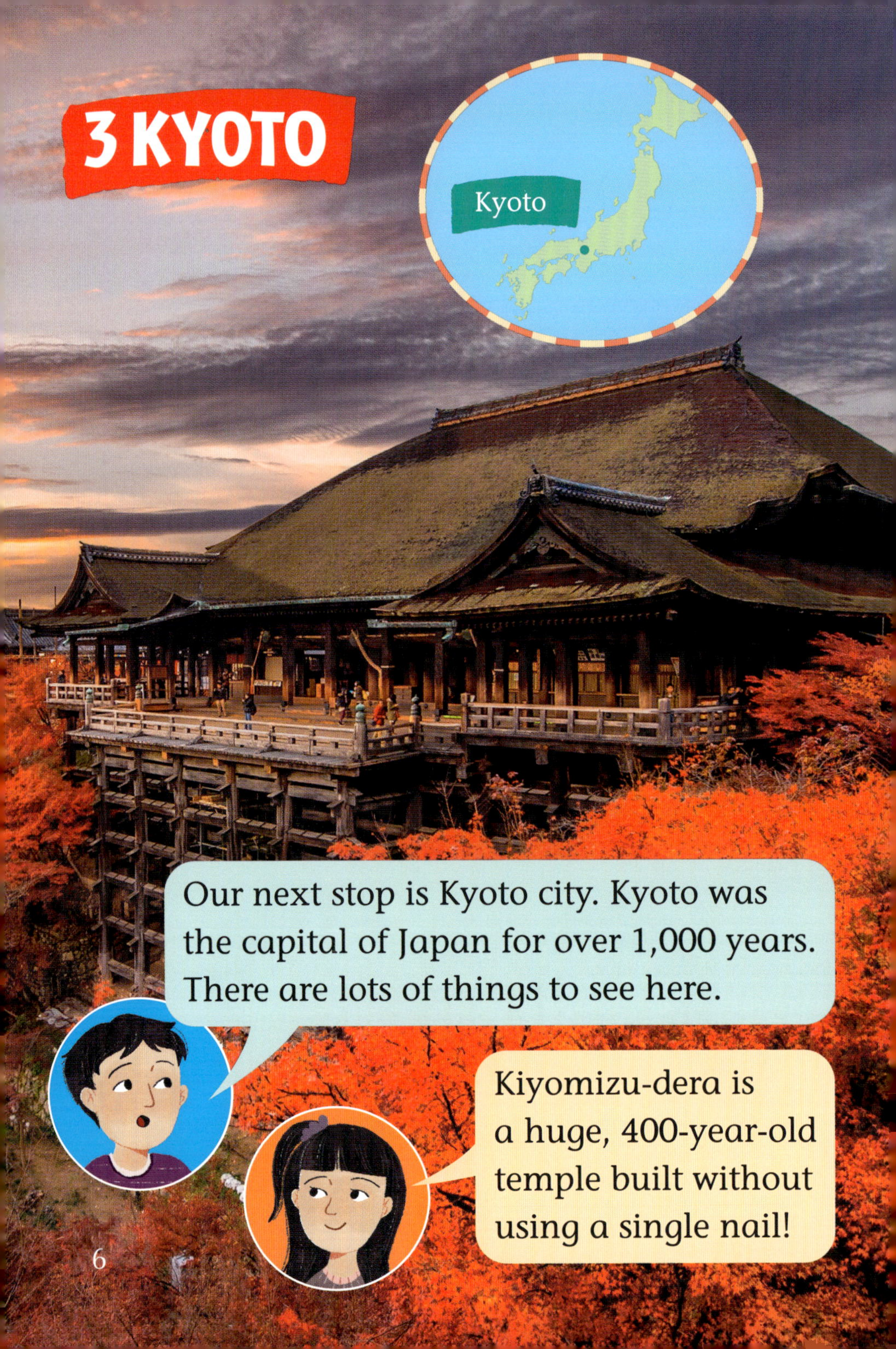
Kyoto
Our next stop is Kyoto city. Kyoto was the capital of Japan for over 1,000 years. There are lots of things to see here.
Kiyomizu-dera is a huge, 400-year-old temple built without using a single nail!

Ninomaru Palace, a 400-year-old building within Nijo Castle, is beautiful. It has "nightingale floors" which chirp like birds when you walk on them!

The walls are covered in **gold leaf**, then painted.

# 4 SHIZUOKA

Shizuoka

We're now in Shizuoka, looking at Mount Fuji, Japan's most famous mountain. Mount Fuji is Japan's tallest mountain and an active volcano, but it hasn't **erupted** for over 300 years!

Shizuoka is also famous for producing almost half of all the tea grown in Japan.

tea **plantation**

Mount Fuji
Time for some green ice cream!
It's made with powdered green tea, called matcha.

# 5 TOKYO

Next, we're going to Tokyo. In the past, Tokyo was called Edo, but it was renamed when it became the capital city in 1868.

Tokyo is a very **high-tech** city. There are even hotels where robots greet and help the guests!

Look, robot **receptionists**. They seem almost human!

This dinosaur assistant is better.

Tokyo
Tokyo has many **historic** buildings.
It has modern ones too – including the tallest tower in the world, Tokyo Skytree!

# 6 FOOD

It's time to stop for some food. These are my favourites ...

unagi: barbecued eel on rice

onigiri: rice-balls stuffed with different fillings and wrapped in nori seaweed

doryaki: small pancakes sandwiched with a sweet red-bean filling

Remember to say "itadaki-masu" before you eat, to give thanks for the food!

Many restaurants have a display of the food they serve.
If you can't read the menu, you can point to the plastic food!
てっちり
1,680円
豚しゃぶ
1,680円
(税込 1,764円)
黒毛和牛しゃぶ
1,980円
(税込 2,079円)
おぼろ豆富
がんこ豆富盛合せ
580円(税込 609円)
大根パリパリサラダ
580円
大海老サラダ
880円
若鶏唐揚げ
680円
いか照り焼き
580円
焼き鳥
380円
串かつ盛合せ
680円
なす二色田楽
580円
白魚チーズ揚げ
580円
海老天ぷら
580円
がんこ御膳
すし松膳
50周年
生本まぐろ造り膳
1,980円(税込 2,079円)
天ざるねぎとろ定食
980円(税込1,029円)

# 7 NAGANO

Nagano is an area located in a mountain range known as the "Japanese Alps".

If you visit Nagano in winter, you can learn to ski.

Snow monkeys live here. They stay warm by bathing in an outdoor onsen in the forest!

Many people go to hot spring resorts to relax in an onsen bath too.

# 8 NIIGATA

Niigata
Now we're heading to an area famous for growing rice, and for the spectacular Nagaoka Fireworks Festival.
Over 20,000 fireworks are set off each evening for two days!

Some Japanese people eat rice with every meal.
Rice is used to make all sorts of snacks too, both sweet and savoury … like these rice crackers. They're crunchy and salty.

# 9 HOKKAIDO



We are now in Hokkaido, an island on the northern tip of Japan. The summers are warm, and farmers can grow lots of things in the rich soil.

But the winters are cold, and it can be snowy from November to May.

Sapporo, the biggest city in Hokkaido, is one of the snowiest cities in the world!
In February, there is a snow and ice festival. Look at these sculptures!

# 10 HIGH SPEED TRAVEL

## GLOSSARY

**erupted** become active

**gold leaf** tissue-thin sheets of pure gold

**high-tech** with very advanced computers and equipment

**historic** something old that is famous or important

**hot springs** sources of hot water naturally heated underground

**plantation** fields where plants are farmed

**receptionists** hotel workers who help you as you arrive

**tatami mats** traditional indoor floor, woven using a special type of dried grass

## INDEX

# EXPLORE JAPAN

Kyoto

Kyushu

Beppu

Sapporo
Hokkaido
Nagano
Niigata
Tokyo
Shizuoka

# Ideas for reading

Written by Gill Matthews
*Primary Literacy Consultant*

**Reading objectives:**
- draw on what they already know or on background information and vocabulary provided by the teacher
- make inferences on the basis of what is being said and done
- answer and ask questions
- participate in discussion about books, poems and other works that are read to them and those that they can read for themselves, taking turns and listening to what others say

**Spoken language objectives:**
- maintain attention and participate actively in collaborative conversations, staying on topic and initiating and responding to comments
- use spoken language to develop understanding through speculating, hypothesising, imagining and exploring ideas
- participate in discussions, presentations, performances, role play, improvisations and debates

**Curriculum links:** Relationships education: respectful relationships

**Interest words:** onsen, unagi, onigiri, dorayaki, itadaki-masu

**Word count:** 708

## Build a context for reading

- Ask children to read the title of the book and to look closely at the front cover.
- Discuss what they can see on the cover.
- Read the back-cover blurb. Explore what the children know about Japan. Ask what they think they will find out from the book.
- Point out that this is an information book. Discuss the features that the children think they will find in the book.
- Note that Japanese words written in the English alphabet are pronounced as they would be in English. Encourage children to think about how they would pronounce the words phonetically.

## Understand and apply reading strategies

- Challenge the children to find the contents page. Discuss the purpose and organisation of a contents.